COUNTRY 🌐 PROFILES

HAITI

BY ALICIA Z. KLEPEIS

BELLWETHER MEDIA • MINNEAPOLIS, MN

Blastoff! Discovery launches a new mission: reading to learn. Filled with facts and features, each book offers you an exciting new world to explore!

This edition first published in 2020 by Bellwether Media, Inc.

No part of this publication may be reproduced in whole or in part without written permission of the publisher.
For information regarding permission, write to Bellwether Media, Inc.,
Attention: Permissions Department,
6012 Blue Circle Drive, Minnetonka, MN 55343.

Library of Congress Cataloging-in-Publication Data

Names: Klepeis, Alicia Z., author.
Title: Haiti / by Alicia Z. Klepeis.
Description: Minneapolis, MN : Bellwether Media, Inc., [2020] |
    Series: Blastoff! Discovery: Country Profiles | Includes
    bibliographical references and index. | Audience: Grades 4-6 |
Audience: Ages 7-13 | Summary: "Engaging images accompany
    information about Haiti. The combination of high-interest subject
    matter and narrative text is intended for students in grades 3 through
    8" – Provided by publisher.
Identifiers: LCCN 2019035665 (print) | LCCN 2019035666
    (ebook) | ISBN 9781644871683 (library binding) |
    ISBN 9781618918444 (ebook)
Subjects: LCSH: Haiti–Juvenile literature.
Classification: LCC F1915.2 .K55 2020 (print) | LCC F1915.2
    (ebook) | DDC 972.94–dc23
LC record available at https://lccn.loc.gov/2019035665
LC ebook record available at https://lccn.loc.gov/2019035666

Editor: Rebecca Sabelko   Designer: Brittany McIntosh

Printed in the United States of America, North Mankato, MN.

TABLE OF CONTENTS

It is a mild spring afternoon in Macaya National Park. A group of **tourists** prepares to explore this natural wonderland. Through the **cloud forest**, they spot the 7,700-foot-high (2,347-meter-high) high Pic Macaya reaching into the sky.

OTHER TOP SITES

BASSIN BLEU

CAP-HAÏTIEN CATHEDRAL

CITADELLE LAFERRIÈRE

LA VISITE NATIONAL PARK

The visitors hike among the park's ferns and mosses. Many stop to photograph the incredible variety of colorful orchids. In the late afternoon, the group treks deeper into the forest. They hear frogs croaking. A small anole lizard darts across a leaf in search of a tasty insect to eat. Welcome to Haiti!

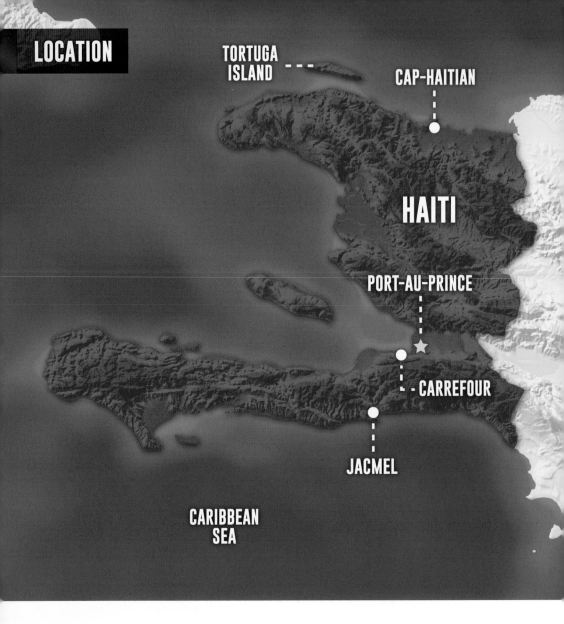

TORTUGA
ISLAND

CAP-HAITIAN

HAITI

PORT-AU-PRINCE

CARREFOUR

JACMEL

CARIBBEAN
SEA

Haiti is located in the Caribbean on the island of Hispanola. It occupies the western third of the island. Its neighbor to the east is the Dominican Republic. Waves from the Atlantic Ocean lap against the northern shores of Haiti. The waves of the Caribbean Sea wash against the country's western and southern coasts.

ATLANTIC
OCEAN

THE
DOMINICAN REPUBLIC

AHOY, MATEY!

Off the coast of Haiti, Tortuga Island was once a pirate hideout! In the 1600s, the rough adventurers used the island to protect their valuable loot.

N
W + E
S

Haiti covers 10,714 square miles (27,750 square kilometers). The nation's capital, Port-au-Prince, lies on the west coast. Port-au-Prince has many **communes** including Carrefour. These territories are extensions of the capital city with huge numbers of residents.

LANDSCAPE AND CLIMATE

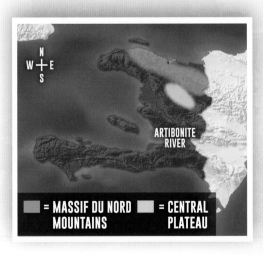

ARTIBONITE RIVER

= MASSIF DU NORD MOUNTAINS   = CENTRAL PLATEAU

Haiti is a country with rough **terrain**. Warm ocean waters crash upon the steep cliffs of the nation's rocky shoreline. The **Massif** du Nord range runs along the northern **peninsula**. The longest of Haiti's many rivers is the Artibonite. It flows from the Dominican Republic to the Caribbean Sea between Haiti's mountain ranges. The heavily populated Central **Plateau** provides a break between the northern mountains and those that fill the southern peninsula.

ARTIBONITE RIVER

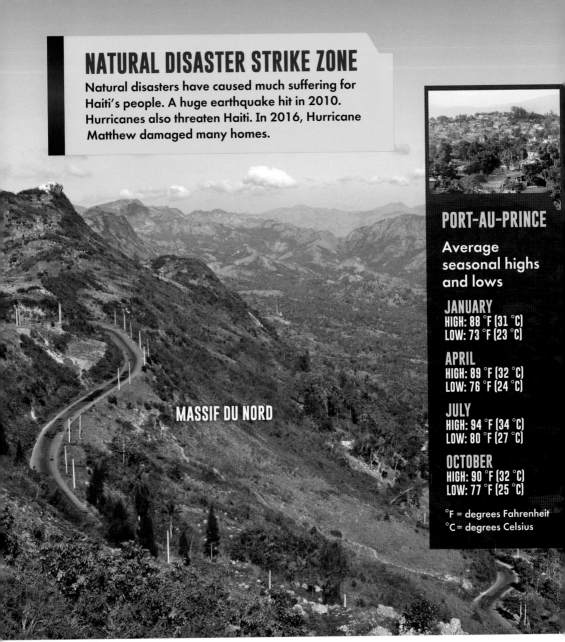

NATURAL DISASTER STRIKE ZONE

Natural disasters have caused much suffering for Haiti's people. A huge earthquake hit in 2010. Hurricanes also threaten Haiti. In 2016, Hurricane Matthew damaged many homes.

MASSIF DU NORD

PORT-AU-PRINCE

Average seasonal highs and lows

JANUARY
HIGH: 88 °F (31 °C)
LOW: 73 °F (23 °C)

APRIL
HIGH: 89 °F (32 °C)
LOW: 76 °F (24 °C)

JULY
HIGH: 94 °F (34 °C)
LOW: 80 °F (27 °C)

OCTOBER
HIGH: 90 °F (32 °C)
LOW: 77 °F (25 °C)

°F = degrees Fahrenheit
°C = degrees Celsius

Haiti has a **tropical** climate. Temperatures are warm nearly all year long. Some regions receive rainfall from May to November. Other parts of Haiti have two rainy seasons each year.

MANATEE

Haiti is home to a wide variety of wildlife! Dolphins and manatees swim in the warm waters off the country's coasts. Snail-like conches feed on plants in the shallow waters. Crocodiles and lizards dwell in and around the rivers of Haiti's southern peninsula. Greater bulldog bats are one of Haiti's few mammals. They have adapted to eat fish.

QUEEN CONCH

Haiti is a birdwatcher's paradise! The Hispaniolan emerald flits about in search of nectar high within mountain forests. The national bird, the Hispaniolan trogon, makes its home in the southern mountains. Flamingoes feed and roost on the island of Gonâve.

GREATER BULLDOG BAT

HISPANIOLAN EMERALD

HISPANIOLAN TROGON

AMERICAN
FLAMINGO

AMERICAN FLAMINGO

Life Span: 20 to 30 years
Red List Status: least concern

American flamingo range = ▮

LEAST CONCERN	NEAR THREATENED	VULNERABLE	ENDANGERED	CRITICALLY ENDANGERED	EXTINCT IN THE WILD	EXTINCT
▲						

Over 10 million people live in Haiti. More than nine out of ten people are the **descendants** of African people brought to Hispaniola as **slaves**. Some people belonging to **minority** groups in Haiti are of mixed African and European descent. Others have only European **ancestors**.

More than half of all Haitians belong to the Roman Catholic Church. Others practice different forms of Christianity. A small number of Haitians practice other religions, including vodou. Vodou includes certain Catholic **rituals**. But it also has its own special ceremonies. The official languages of Haiti are French and Creole.

FAMOUS FACE

Name: Wyclef Jean
Birthday: October 17, 1969
Hometown: Croix-des-Bouquets, Haiti
Famous for: A popular rapper and music producer who has won three Grammy Awards, including Best Rap Album with his band, The Fugees

SPEAK CREOLE

PORT-AU-PRINCE

ENGLISH	CREOLE	HOW TO SAY IT
hello	bonjou	BOHN-joo
goodbye	babay	bah-bye
please	souple	SOOP-lee
thank you	mèsi	meh-SEE
yes	wi	wee
no	non	no

Just over half of all Haitians live in **urban** areas such as Port-au-Prince. People often live in crowded **slums**. Most city dwellers do not have access to electricity or running water. City travel is often on foot.

COLORFUL TRAVEL

A common form of transportation in Haiti is the tap-tap. Tap-taps can be buses or pickup trucks. They are famous for their colorful and artsy designs. Tap-taps are cheap and fun ways to get around!

TAP-TAP
PORT-AU-PRINCE

COMPOUND

Most **rural** homes are made of mud with **thatched roofs**. Houses are typically clustered in **compounds**. Normally the men in these compounds are related. People in villages usually travel on foot or by bicycle.

Family is very important to Haitians. Grandparents may help out with childcare when mothers or fathers are working. Urban families usually have fewer children than rural ones.

The phrase *pa gen pwoblèm*, meaning "no have problem," is often used in Haiti. It is used to describe the way people appreciate what they have. Haitians use the term to reply to a thank-you, avoid an awkward silence, or just express that life is good.

Haitians enjoy listening to music and dancing in their free time. One popular style of music is called *méringue*. It blends European dance music from the 1800s and drum rhythms from Africa. Méringue musicians play stringed instruments and *tamburas*, or two-headed drums. Méringue dancing is fast and fun.

RARA

ROARIN' RARA

Rara is a festival, a season, a type of music, a kind of dance, and a ritual all at once! Its songs often celebrate the African roots of Haiti's people. Performers play Haitian instruments including bamboo trumpets.

17

Haiti provides free schooling to every child beginning at age 6. But many schools are private and cost money. There are also not enough teachers or schools in Haiti. Many children do not even complete primary school. But the nation's people are hopeful for change in the future.

About half of all Haitians have **service jobs**. Some people sell goods and food in markets. Others work in hospitals and schools. Haitians also **manufacture** products like clothing and footwear. Farmers grow **cassava**, bananas, rice, and coffee beans. Mangoes are a big moneymaker. Farmers also raise livestock including goats and cattle.

MORE CLEAN ENERGY

Haiti is looking to increase its renewable energy production. Wind and solar power might be usable green energy sources in the future.

SOCCER

The most popular sport in Haiti is soccer. Haitian girls and boys often start playing soccer from a young age. Basketball is also growing in popularity. Men enjoy playing card games and dominoes in their free time. Women tend to socialize by telling stories and jokes. Haitian children play many games including marbles and jacks. They also play many versions of tag.

MARBLES

Listening to music is a popular pastime in Haiti. Young Haitians enjoy dancing in nightclubs. More middle-class people are also able to afford televisions. Some people watch movies on their smartphones.

DOMINOES

HAITIAN METALWORK

Detailed metalwork is a popular craft from Haiti. It often features trees, animals, and people.

What You Need:
- paper
- a pencil
- scissors
- heavy-duty aluminum foil
- a permanent marker

Instructions:
1. Look online or in books to see some examples of Haitian metalwork.

2. Using your paper and pencil, sketch out a sample design for your metalwork. Use your scissors to cut around the outer edge of your sketch. Set your sketch aside.

3. Roll out as much foil as you need to fit your sketch. Cut it from the roll.

4. Place your sketch onto your aluminum foil. Trace around the edges of your sketch on the foil with the permanent marker.

5. Cut the foil to create your metalwork. Enjoy!

People in Haiti cook with many spices. They often use hot peppers and garlic in their dishes. Popular fruits include citrus fruits, mangoes, and avocados. Meat is not eaten much, as it is expensive.

Breakfast can be coffee and bread with jam and butter. Some people have heartier breakfasts such as corn and codfish or plantains and liver. Haitians eat rice and beans on a daily basis. Stews are also eaten often. *Soup joumou* has a base of beef stock and stewed pumpkin. *Poulet creole*, a dish combining chicken, tomatoes, and spices, is popular in the north.

SOUP JOUMOU

POULET CREOLE

RED BEANS AND RICE

This hearty dish is a simple but typical Haitian meal. Have an adult help you with this recipe.

Ingredients:
2 1/2 cups chicken or vegetable broth
1 15-ounce can kidney beans, drained
1 cup unsweetened coconut milk
1/4 teaspoon allspice
1/2 teaspoon dried thyme
1 cup white rice

Steps:
1. Add 2 cups broth, kidney beans, coconut milk, allspice, and thyme into a heavy saucepan.

2. Bring this mixture to a boil, then stir in the rice.

3. Turn the heat down to low. Simmer the mixture uncovered, stirring often, until nearly all of the liquid is absorbed. The rice should be creamy and soft. This will take about 20 minutes. If the mixture seems dry, add the remaining broth. Enjoy!

CELEBRATIONS

CARNIVAL

FÈT GEDE

November 2 is *Fèt Gede* in Haiti. On this night,
Haitians honor the lives of the dead. People visit
their ancestors in cemeteries. They also have
parties with music and food.

People in Haiti celebrate many holidays. January 1 is New Year's and Independence Day! Haitians visit friends and family to share good wishes for the upcoming year. Carnival is Haiti's biggest celebration. It takes place in January or February just before Lent. Colorful parades take place across the country. People dance and play music. Some even dress as monsters called *chaloskas*.

May 18 is Flag Day. People dress in bright red or blue, the colors of the Haitian flag. Many towns and cities hold parades. The people of Haiti celebrate their **culture** and country throughout the year!

FLAG DAY

AROUND 400 TO 250 BCE
Earliest known occupation of Hispaniola by the native Taíno people

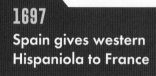

1697
Spain gives western Hispaniola to France

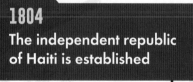

1804
The independent republic of Haiti is established

1492
Christopher Columbus lands on the island of Hispaniola

1801
Former slave Toussaint Louverture conquers Haiti and ends slavery

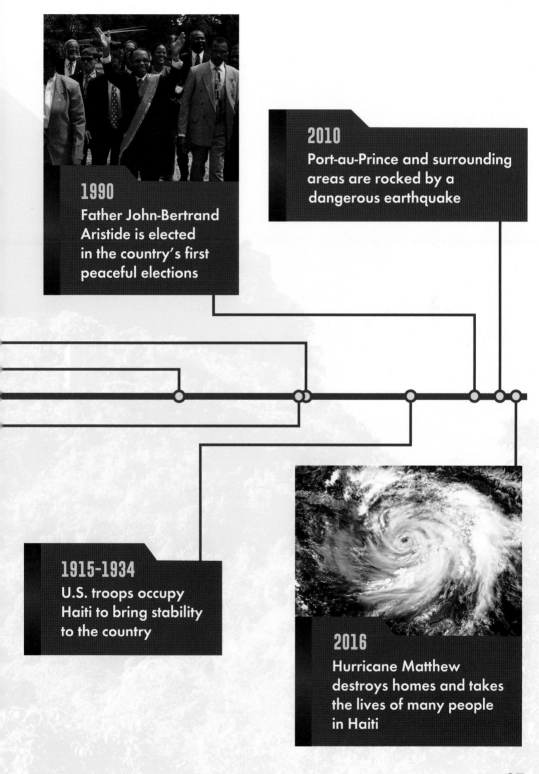

1990
Father John-Bertrand Aristide is elected in the country's first peaceful elections

2010
Port-au-Prince and surrounding areas are rocked by a dangerous earthquake

1915-1934
U.S. troops occupy Haiti to bring stability to the country

2016
Hurricane Matthew destroys homes and takes the lives of many people in Haiti

HAITI FACTS

Official Name: Republic of Haiti

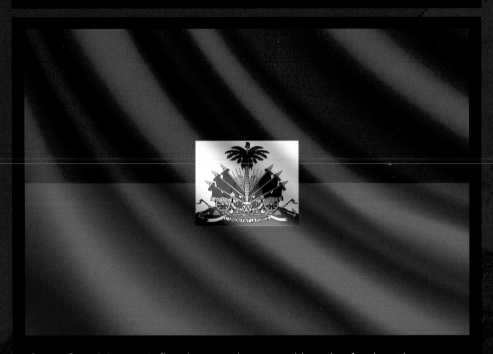

Flag of Haiti: Haiti's flag has two horizontal bands of color. The top band is blue, and the bottom is red. In the center is a white rectangle featuring the coat of arms. This coat of arms has a palm tree, flags, and two cannons. A scroll below the cannons has the nation's motto "*L'Union Fait La Force*," meaning Union Makes Strength.

Area: 10,714 square miles (27,750 square kilometers)

Capital City: Port-au-Prince

Important Cities: Carrefour, Jacmel, Pétionville, Cap-Haitian

Population: 10,788,440 (July 2018)

WHERE PEOPLE LIVE

COUNTRYSIDE
44.7%

CITY
55.3%

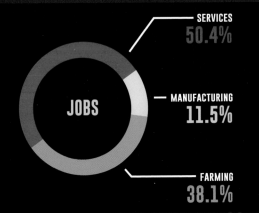

JOBS

SERVICES
50.4%

MANUFACTURING
11.5%

FARMING
38.1%

Main Exports:

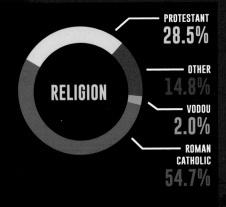

clothing   coffee   tropical fruit

cocoa beans   essential oils

National Holiday:
Independence Day (January 1)

Main Languages:
French and Creole

Form of Government:
semi-presidential republic

Title for Country Leaders:
prime minister (head of government),
president (head of state)

RELIGION

PROTESTANT
28.5%

OTHER
14.8%

VODOU
2.0%

ROMAN CATHOLIC
54.7%

Unit of Money:
gourde (HTG)

GLOSSARY

ancestors—relatives who lived long ago

cassava—a tropical plant with starchy, edible roots

cloud forest—a wet mountain forest located in a warm area, often with many clouds

communes—divisions of local government; Haiti's communes are extensions of the capital city with huge numbers of residents.

compounds—enclosed areas that include groups of buildings

culture—the beliefs, arts, and ways of life in a place or society

descendants—people related to a person or group of people who lived at an earlier time

manufacture—to make products, often with machines

massif—a tightly packed group of mountains

minority—related to a group of people who are different from a larger group in a country

peninsula—a section of land that extends out from a larger piece of land and is almost completely surrounded by water

plateau—an area of flat, raised land

rituals—religious ceremonies or practices

rural—related to the countryside

service jobs—jobs that perform tasks for people or businesses

slaves—people who work for no pay and are considered property

slums—parts of cities that are crowded and have poor housing

terrain—the surface features of an area of land

thatched roofs—roofs with coverings made of grass or straw

tourists—people who travel to visit another place

tropical—part of the tropics; the tropics is a hot, rainy region near the equator.

urban—related to cities and city life

TO LEARN MORE

AT THE LIBRARY

Rechner, Amy. *The Dominican Republic*. Minneapolis, Minn.: Bellwether Media, 2019.

Sonneborn, Liz. *Haiti*. New York, N.Y.: Children's Press, 2019.

Wiseman, Blaine. *Haiti*. New York, N.Y.: AV2 by Weigl, 2018.

ON THE WEB

FACTSURFER

Factsurfer.com gives you a safe, fun way to find more information.

1. Go to www.factsurfer.com.

2. Enter "Haiti" into the search box and click 🔍.

3. Select your book cover to see a list of related web sites.

INDEX